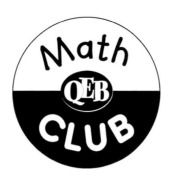

Using Numbers Book 2

Ann Montague-Smith

QEB Publishing

Published in the United States by
QEB Publishing, Inc.
23062 La Cadena Drive
Laguna Hills, CA 92653

www.qeb-publishing.com

Library of Congress Control Number: 2005921277

ISBN 1-59566-113-1

Written by Ann Montague–Smith
Designed and edited by The Complete Works
Illustrated by Peter Lawson
Photography by Steve Lumb

Publisher Steve Evans
Creative Director Louise Morley
Editorial Manager Jean Coppendale

Printed and bound in China

Contents

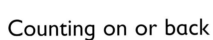

Numbers to 100

Play this game with a friend. Take turns to throw a small coin onto the spinner. Move your counter along the windows of the buildings. Say the number you land on out loud.

Start

1	2	3	4
5	6	7	8
9	10	11	12
13	14	15	16
17	18	19	20
21	22		

23	24	25
26	27	28
29	30	31
32	33	34
35	36	37

38	39	40	41
42	43	44	45
46	47	48	49
50	51	52	53
54	55	56	57
		58	59
		60	61

Take turns to point to any number.
Ask your friend to say it.

1 2
3 4

Try this

With a friend, take turns saying a number between 1 and 99. Now decide whether to count up to 100 from that number, or down to 0. Now write that number, and the next nine numbers, in order.

> Start at 45 and count back.

62 63 64 65

66 67 68 69

70 71 72 73

74 75 76 77

78 79 80 81

82 83 84 85

86 87 88 89

90 91 92 93

94 95 96 97

98 99 100

Finish

5

Counting to 100

The dogs have spilled paint on the number strips.
Can you find out which numbers are missing?

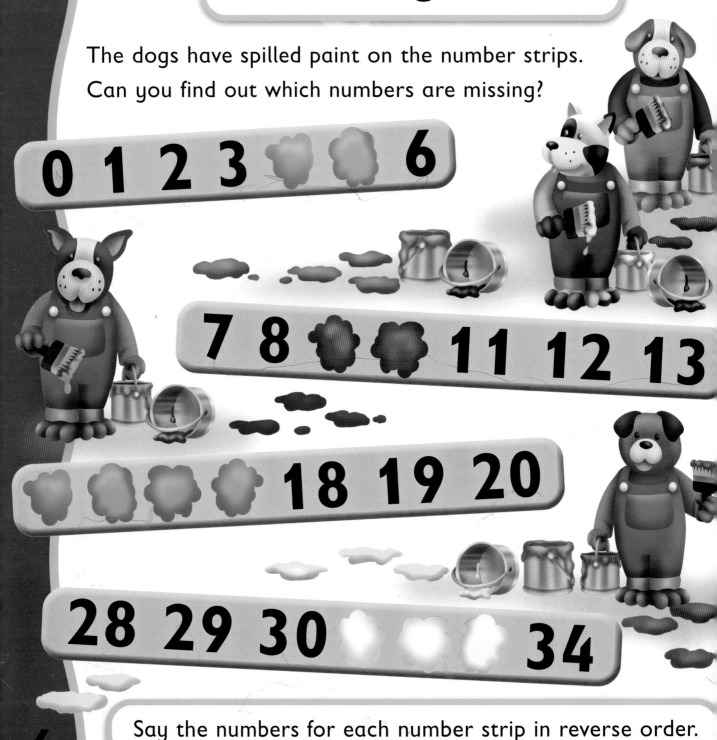

0 1 2 3 ░ ░ 6

7 8 ░ ░ 11 12 13

░ ░ ░ ░ 18 19 20

28 29 30 ░ ░ ░ 34

Say the numbers for each number strip in reverse order.

6

Now try this

Say all the numbers from 0 to 100. Now count backward, starting with 100, 99, 98...

100, 99, 98, 97, 96, 95, 94 ...

50

62 63 64 **67**

79 **84**

90 **93**

95 **98** **100**

7

Double digits

Match the double-digit balloons to the items of food below.

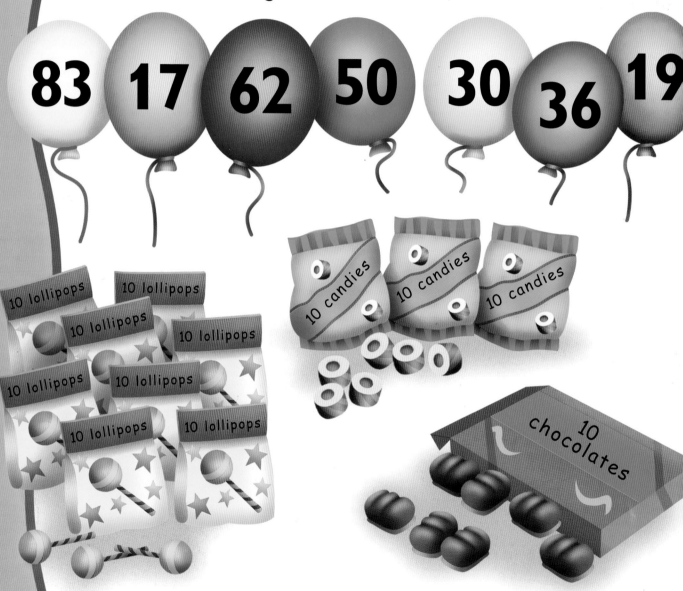

83 17 62 50 30 36 19

10 lollipops
10 lollipops
10 lollipops
10 lollipops
10 lollipops
10 lollipops
10 lollipops
10 lollipops

10 candies
10 candies
10 candies

10 chocolates

Which is the largest double-digit number?
Which is the smallest?

10 cookies

10 cookies

10 cookies

10 cookies

10 cookies

10 cookies

Double-digit numbers have a tens place and a ones place, and can be written like this: 34=30+4. Think of five more and write them out.

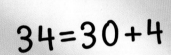

$$34=30+4$$

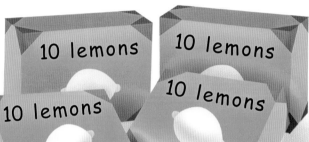

10 lemons

10 lemons

10 lemons

10 lemons

10 lemons

10 cupcakes

10 cupcakes

10 apples

10 cupcakes

9

Counting on or back

Choose a number from the mat below. Count on from that number to 100, then back again.

1	2	3	4	5
11	12	13	14	1.
21	22	23	24	2
31	32	33	34	3.
41	42	43	44	4.
51	52	53	54	5.
61	62	63	64	6
71	72	73	74	7
81	82	83	84	8
91	92	93	94	9.

Choose some more numbers and do it again.

Challenge

Count on from 100.
How far can you count?
Can you count back to 100?

100, 101, 102, 103, 104, 105, 106...

6	7	8	9	10
6	17	18	19	20
26	27	28	29	30
36	37	38	39	40
46	47	48	49	50
56	57	58	59	60
66	67	68	69	70
76	77	78	79	80
86	87	88	89	90
96	97	98	99	100

11

Ordering numbers to 100

Some of the t-shirts have lost their numbers.
Look at the numbers on the ground.
Which numbers will fit into the spaces on the t-shirts?

55 67 1 46 15

12

Which number will not fit? Can you explain why?

Try this

You will need a deck of cards.
Take out the picture cards.
Take 2 number cards. Make a
double-digit number with them. Now
make another double-digit number
with your cards. Write as many
numbers as you can that will fall
between your 2 numbers.

29

37

41

84

22

60

5

73

49

18

50

More or less

Read the numbers on the labels. Say the number that is 1 more than each number. Now say the number that is 1 less than each number.

Do this again, but say the number that is 10 more, and then 10 less.

51

36

Challenge

Write down any number between 30 and 80. Now write down the number that is 20 more. Write down the number that is 20 less. Now write all your numbers in order, starting with the smallest number.

18 38 58

72

48

87

15

Missing numbers

Some numbers have fallen off the hundred square that Gerry Giraffe is holding. Which ones? Compare to the full hundred square opposite.

	2	3	4
11	12	13	14
21	22	23	24
	32	33	

Bear's square:

5	6	7	8
15	16	17	18
	26	27	
	36	37	
		47	

Elephant's square:

31			
41	42	43	44
51		53	
61	62	63	

Lion's square:

	83			
92	93	94	95	96	97

Now look at the pieces of square the other animals are holding. Figure out which numbers are missing.

Now try this

Mark with a pencil a 10 by 10 grid on some squared paper. Write 1 in the top left-hand corner square, and 100 in the bottom right-hand corner square. Take turns to write in any number on the grid until all the numbers from 1 to 100 are there in order.

64	65
72	73	74	75
81	82	84	85

1	2	3	4	5	6	7	8	9	10
11	12	13	14	15	16	17	18	19	20
21	22	23	24	25	26	27	28	29	30
31	32	33	34	35	36	37	38	39	40
41	42	43	44	45	46	47	48	49	50
51	52	53	54	55	56	57	58	59	60
61	62	63	64	65	66	67	68	69	70
71	72	73	74	75	76	77	78	79	80
81	82	83	84	85	86	87	88	89	90
91	92	93	94	95	96	97	98	99	100

45	46
55	56	57	58
	66	67	68
		77	78
		87	88

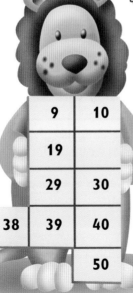

9	10
19	
29	30
38	39	40
		50

48	49
	59
	69	70
		80
	89	90
98	99	100

17

Rounding

Numbers ending with 1–4 get rounded down to the nearest 10. Numbers ending with 5–9 get rounded up to the nearest 10. Round the numbers on the apples.

86

75

6

31

91

47

36

53

99

98

Write all the numbers on the apples in correct number order. Underneath each number, write the number it will round off to.

18

Now try this

This girl wants to buy 35 jellybeans to share with the children in her class. The jellybeans come in packs of 10. How many packs must she buy? What if there were 32 children in her class? How many packs of jellybeans would she need now? Explain your answer to a friend.

82

57

14

65

78

43

19

24

92

84

Path problem

The numbers on the path must be painted on. The first stone reads "1." The last slab will read "99," so this will need two 9s to be painted. How many number 1s need to be painted? How many number 2s, 3s, 4s, 5s, 6s, 7s, 8s, and 9s?

Can you find a quick way to work this out?

Challenge

What if the numbers went from 51 to 150? How many of each single digit would be needed?

10

9

8

7

90

91

92

93

94

95

96

97

98

99

Supporting notes

Numbers to 100, pages 4–5

Encourage children to read numbers and write them. Point to any number and check that the children can read it. If they are unsure, discuss the tens place value, then the ones, then the whole number, so that the child begins to understand how the number is made up.

Counting to 100, pages 6–7

If children are unsure about numbers larger than about 30, count together from 0 to 100 and back again, several times. Now point to the numbers on the page and read these together so the children become more confident with the numbers before tackling the work.

Double digits, pages 8–9

In addition to being able to read and write double-digit numbers, children need to understand what each of the place values stands for. If children are unsure about this, read the tens and ones numbers in two ways. For example, take 25: 2 tens and 5 ones is the same as twenty-five.

Counting on or back, pages 10–11

If children are unsure about counting to 100, they can make mistakes such as twenty-nine, twenty-ten, twenty-eleven. Check that the children understand what to say at the decade change: 29, 30… 39, 40… etc.

Ordering numbers to 100, pages 12–13

If children are not confident about which numbers fill in the spaces, count on from the smaller number to the larger number. This will help children to realize which numbers fit.

More or less, pages 14–15

If children find this activity difficult, ask them to write out the numbers from 1 to 100, or do this for them, in a grid with 1–10 along the first line, 11–20 along the next, etc., lining up the numbers. Use this to find the 1 more and 1 less numbers, then the 10 more and 10 less numbers. Ask "What do you notice about 10 more? And 10 less? Where do these come on the grid?"

Missing numbers, pages 16–17

Children may find it easier to tackle this activity with a hundred square grid, with 1 in the top left-hand corner, and 100 in the bottom right-hand corner. When they are confident ng this, ask them to try the activity again, this time without looking at the hundred square grid.

Rounding, pages 18–19

As long as children understand the convention that single digits of 5–9 round up, and 1–4 round down, rounding is easy. If children find it difficult, suggest that they write the numbers 1 to 9 in order, and draw a line between 4 and 5. They can use the line to help them remember which numbers round up, and which down.

Path problem, pages 20–21

Twenty of each of 1, 2, 3…9 will be needed. Discourage children from just counting each digit. Instead, suggest that they look at the numbers 1–9, then 11–20, then 21–30, to see how many of each digit is used. Encourage them to predict what they notice about the overall total for each digit.

23

Using this book

The illustrations in this book are bright, cheerful, and colorful, and are designed to capture children's interest. Sit somewhere comfortable together as you look at the book. Children of this age will normally be able to read most of the instructional words. Help with the reading where necessary, so all children can take part in the activities, regardless of how fluent they are at reading.

The activities in this book will extend children's knowledge about numbers, from numbers to 30 and numbers up to 100. Children will begin to understand how individual digits combine to make a number, such as 3 and 5 can make 35, and can also make 53. What matters is where each digit is placed, and whether it is in the tens or ones place. If children are unsure about this, give more help with reading numbers. For example, use a deck of cards with the digits 0 to 9. Ask the children to choose two cards and make a double-digit number, such as 45 with a 4 and a 5 card. Ask them to read the number. Now ask them to reverse the digits and to say what number they now have: 54. This could become a game, where one child shows a double-digit number, and another child says the other number that could be made with the same digits.

Encourage the children to explain how they found the answers to the questions. Being able to explain their thinking, and to use the correct mathematical vocabulary, helps children clarify in their minds what they have just done. Also, for children who are not so sure of how to solve the problem, hearing what others did, and how they did it, helps them to use the methods more effectively.

Encourage children to make notes as they work at an activity. They can record numbers, writing them in order, or write simple sentences to explain what they did. Encourage them to be systematic in the way they work, so they do not miss a vital part of the evidence they need to find a solution.

Above all, enjoy the mathematical games, activities, and challenges in this book together!